Full Throttle

Mustang

Tracy Maurer

Rourke
Publishing LLC
Vero Beach, Florida 32964

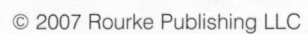

AUTHOR CREDITS:
The author gratefully acknowledges project assistance provided by Chris Edling, and John and Corinn Berken at Forest Lake Ford in Forest Lake, Minnesota.
Also, the author extends appreciation to Mike Maurer, Alan Maurer, Steve Maurer, Matthew Nelson, Lois M. Nelson, Margaret and Thomas, and the team at Rourke. TBD

PHOTO CREDITS: All photos Courtesy of Ford Motor Company

Editor: Robert Stengard-Olliges

Cover design by Todd Field
Page design by Nicola Stratford

Library of Congress Cataloging-in-Publication Data

Maurer, Tracy, 1965-
 Mustang / Tracy Nelson Maurer.
    p. cm. -- (Full throttle)
 Includes index.
 ISBN 1-60044-227-7 (hardcover)
 ISBN 978-1-60044-367-1 (paperback)
 1. Mustang automobile--Juvenile literature. I. Title. II. Series: Maurer, Tracy, 1965-. Full throttle.

TL215.M8M314 2006
629.222'2--dc22   2006017500

Printed in the USA

CG/CG

Rourke Publishing

www.rourkepublishing.com – sales@rourkepublishing.com
Post Office Box 3328, Vero Beach, FL 32964

Table of Contents

Pony Cars

Motoring history shifted into high gear when Ford Motor Company delivered its sporty two-door **Mustang** to dealerships in April 1964. Until then, no other car had blended a stylish and compact four-seat design with powerful engine choices and loads of other options— all at affordable prices.

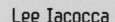

From college students to grandparents, nearly four million gawkers headed to Ford dealerships the first weekend Mustangs were for sale. They bought over 22,000 cars the first day! Mustang became one of the most popular cars of all time.

Lee Iacocca

Car buffs credit Lee Iacocca, a young Ford vice president, for putting backseats into the Mustang. His idea made the sporty car practical for families.

Mustangs started at $2,368. Ford ads claimed it was the "$1-a-pound" car.

Stunned competitors raced to catch up to the Mustang. Soon, all sporty cars with long hoods and short rears were called "pony cars."

mustang
   a wild horse,
   especially in the
   American West

From 1964 to 1968, Ford built more than two million Mustangs and set new sales records.

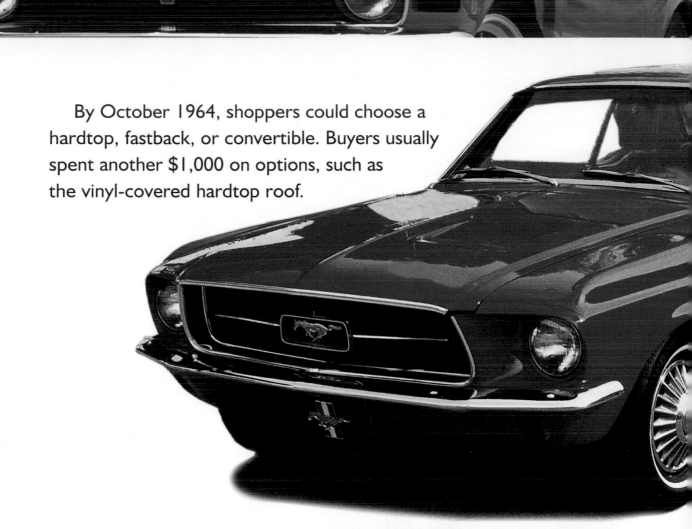

By October 1964, shoppers could choose a hardtop, fastback, or convertible. Buyers usually spent another $1,000 on options, such as the vinyl-covered hardtop roof.

Without side pillars, the hardtop's totally open side windows looked totally cool.

Inside the early Mustang, a sporty three-spoke steering wheel, bucket seats, and a floor-mounted shifter added fresh style.

Pushbutton radios were one of many options.

The 1960s Mustangs came with a choice of engines. They ranged from a small six-cylinder to a big **V-8**. They could accelerate from 0 to 60 miles (97 km) per hour at a pokey 15 seconds or at a breathtaking 6 seconds.

Side "air scoops" from the factory were simply stylish, not functional—until the fastback.

Shelby's Touch

Speed freaks noticed Ford long before the Mustang. In 1962, racer Carroll Shelby dropped a Ford V-8 engine into a lightweight English roadster. His CSX 2000 later became the Ford GT40. It swiped the checkered flag from 1966 to 1969 at the 24 Hours of Le Mans—the first American car to win the European endurance race.

The GT40 wasn't the only Shelby-Ford project that quickly gained fame. Shelby's Cobra Mustangs became the hottest **muscle cars** of the era.

Carroll Shelby used aluminum and fiberglass to rebuild a Mustang fastback into a new breed of racer. His lightweight 1965 GT-350R (R for racing) secured Ford's GT road-racing legacy.

The sleek GT40 earned its name because it measured just 40 inches (88 cm) high.

muscle cars
generally, American cars built between 1964 and 1974 with big engines, two-doors, and back seats

All Shelby Cobra Mustangs started as convertibles or fastbacks.

In the mid 1960s, Hertz rented out 1,000 Shelby Mustang GT-350Hs. These "rent-a-racers" weren't meant for real racing, but many drivers couldn't resist.

Carroll Shelby produced less than 14,500 Mustangs before he stopped in 1970. Among those prized Shelby Mustangs, the 1968 GT500KR (KR = King of the Road) was one of the fastest Mustangs ever.

The GT500KR blew from 0 to 60 miles (97 km) per hour in 6.5 seconds. It finished a quarter mile (425 m) in just 15.0 seconds.

Boss and Mach 1 Mustangs carried on the racing tradition although most muscle cars had lost their appeal by the mid 1970s. Gasoline shortages, high insurance costs due to safety concerns, and poor performance (plus some design duds) shut down muscle cars.

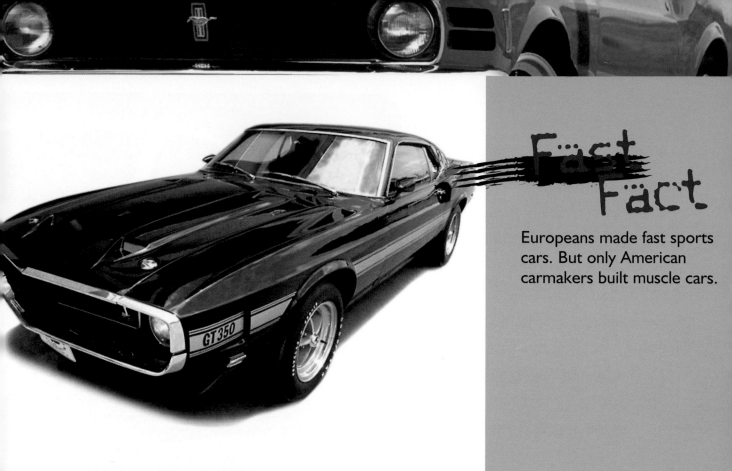

Europeans made fast sports cars. But only American carmakers built muscle cars.

New Again

Ford tinkered with Mustangs over the years. Each generation of the car sparked some interest. In 1981, the Special Vehicle Operations (SVO) group introduced the 1984 SVO Mustang with a surprisingly fast four-cylinder turbocharged engine.

Still, nothing grabbed attention like the original muscle cars did.

Ford changed the SVO into the Special Vehicle Team (SVT) in 1991 to focus on performance cars. These elite engineers studied the best designs from the late 1960s. Today, more than 80,000 high-performance Mustangs have carried the SVT badge. And all fifth-generation Mustangs trace their roots to Carroll Shelby.

The 1994 Mustang SVT Cobra Convertible paced the 1994 Indianapolis 500 race—the first Mustang pace car there since 1979.

coupe
a two-door car, usually with a solid roof

MUSTANG MILESTONES

1964-1973 1st Generation
The first pony cars arrived. Carroll Shelby's Cobra Mustang muscle cars soon followed.

1974-1978 2nd Generation
Mustangs had tame engines but looked sporty (in a polyester-leisure-suit sort of way). Even the 1976 Cobra II Mustang had useless spoilers and a fake hood scoop.

1979-1993 3rd Generation
By 1982, Mustang boosted its power to hit 0 to 60 miles (97 km) per hour in 6.9 seconds. The Mustang convertible came back in 1983 after ten long years.

1994-2004 4th Generation
Style returned and so did performance. Limited-edition retro Shelby-inspired models hinted at the next generation's muscle car revival.

2005 and on... 5th Generation
The Mustang **coupe** and convertible roared with attitude. Then came the double surprise: a return to GT racing and the 2007 Shelby GT500.

The Shift into Fifth

The Mustang GT coupe concept commanded the spotlights at the 2003 North American International Auto Show. Fifth-generation Mustangs sported the long hood and short deck in the pony-car tradition. Inside and out, design cues from the originals saluted the long Mustang heritage. Coupe or convertible? V-6 or GT V-8 upgrade? The choices came back, too!

Fast Fact

The horse on the Mustang grille runs opposite to the way racehorses run on American tracks.

"Pony Package"

The new V-6 Mustang "Pony Package" added the classic red-white-and-blue pony emblem, chrome trim of the 1965 Mustang GT grille, fog lights, and other extras.

2006 "Pony Package" Wheels

For the first time ever, Ford offered 17-inch (43 cm) wheels on its factory-produced V-6 Mustang with the 2006 Pony Package. The wheels looked like the 2005 Mustang GT "Bullitt" wheels.

chassis
the frame that supports the body of a vehicle

Ford engineers gave the fifth-generation Mustang an extra strong **chassis**. They knew that it would have to carry the next big Mustang—the powerful 2007 Shelby Cobra GT500.

Fast Fact

Drivers could choose from 125 colors on their upgraded dashboards.

The Mustang has always been about fun. On some Mustangs, the lights behind the dashboard gauges could change to a different color, depending on the driver's mood. Just for fun.

15

The King Returns

The production model Shelby Cobra GT500 coupe and convertible wowed Mustang fans at the 2006 North American International Auto Show. Carroll Shelby (over 80 years old, trim, and the same feisty mechanical whiz as always) worked with the Ford SVT team to create the new muscle car.

The designers borrowed heavily from Shelby's 1967 and 1968 Cobra Mustangs. Ford planned to build more than half of the new GT500s as hardtops. Rumors hinted that production would stop after about two years or less than 15,000 cars.

Shelby dressed his 1960s high-performance Fords with twin stripes, starting with the roadster that won the Le Mans. "Le Mans stripes" crown the new GT500, too. A lower racing stripe along each side also mimics classic Shelby Mustangs.

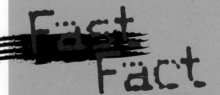

Fast Fact

Contrast stripes started on racecars when factory teams tested look-alike cars.

GT500 Convertible

The Shelby GT500 convertible's stiff chassis helps the car respond better to driver commands. It also sends crash forces away from passengers during an impact.

Rigid chassis designs on convertibles often tip the scales. Ford engineered the strong 2007 Shelby GT500 convertible to outweigh its coupe by less than 125 pounds (275 kg).

The original Shelby GT500 convertible had no Le Mans stripes. Neither does the 2007 Shelby Cobra GT500 Convertible. The new model uses a cloth top instead of the vinyl top on the 2006 Mustang GT convertible.

Fast Fact

Customers can special order unstriped Shelby Cobra GT500s. *But why?*

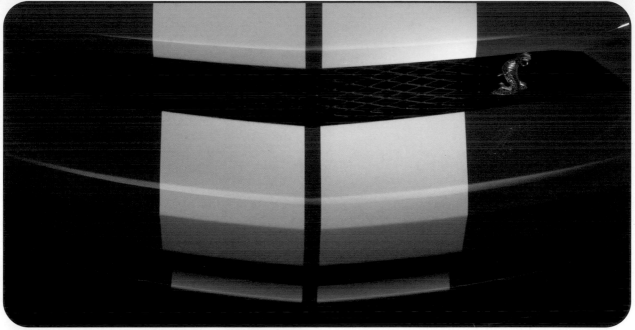

The vintage-styled snake logo replaced the Mustang's usual pony badge on the 2007 Shelby Cobra GT500. It sits to the side on the front grille and accents the centered gas cap under the rear spoiler.

The new Shelby Cobra GT500 leather interior comes in two colors: Charcoal Black or Charcoal Black with Crimson Red on the seats and doors. Satin aluminum accents echo the original's no-nonsense interior.

Engineers swapped the speedometer and tachometer positions from the Mustang GT for the Shelby Cobra GT500.

Early Mustangs hid the gas cap under a round rear badge, just as the 2007 Shelby Cobra GT500 does.

At a Barrett-Jackson auction in January 2006, one lucky bidder paid $600,000 for the right to buy the first 2007 Shelby Cobra GT500. He also took home a nice matching toolbox. The price didn't include the bidder fee, taxes, or the car's price tag. Carroll Shelby's Children's Foundation received the money.

Varooooooooom!

All of today's Mustangs share similar body styles and design treatments that salute the original Shelby Cobras. They look hot. But things *really* sizzle under the hoods. Not one Mustang is a slacker. Even the standard 4.0-liter V-6 Mustang peels out with its game 210 **horsepower**. Next up, the Mustang GT packs a hefty 4.6-liter V-8 with 300 horsepower under the hood. It blasts from 0 to 60 miles (97 km) per hour in 4.9 seconds.

Then there's the Shelby Cobra GT500.

The Shelby Cobra GT500 hits its high speed around 155 miles (248 km) per hour. The supercharged 5.4-liter V-8 conjures over 450 horsepower—the highest rating on a factory-built Ford Mustang ever.

Early Mustangs offered at least four different engines, seven transmissions, four braking setups, and loads of other "extras." Today's options seem simple.

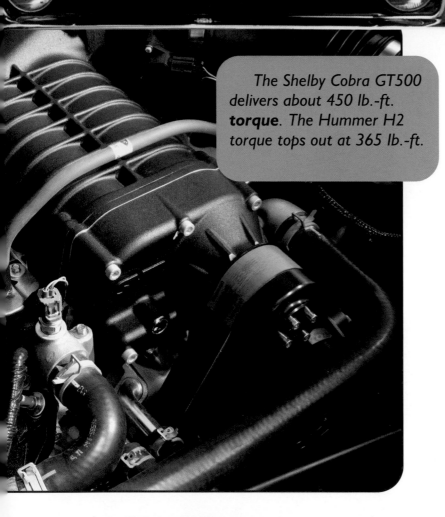

The Shelby Cobra GT500 delivers about 450 lb.-ft. **torque**. The Hummer H2 torque tops out at 365 lb.-ft.

horsepower
> a measure of mechanical power; one horsepower equals 550 pounds (885 kg) lifted at one foot (30.5 cm) per second

torque
> the force that causes an object turn; usually measured in pound-feet (lb-ft)

The Shelby Cobra GT500 borrowed its tire-smoking power from the 2005 Ford GT (another Shelby-inspired speed demon). The Ford GT's supercharged 5.4-liter V-8 engine with a six-speed transmission delivered 550 horsepower. The racy two-seater nailed 3.3 seconds from 0 to 60 miles (97 km) per hour and stomped a quarter-mile run in just 11.6 seconds. Its official top speed was 205 miles (330 km) per hour, although insiders said it went faster.

21

Deep Breathing

A high-performance engine needs to breathe in cool air and exhale its hot air. Using ideas from Shelby's vintage cars, the Ford team gave the Shelby Cobra GT500 super-sized upper and lower grilles to increase airflow. Twin heat **extractors** bulge from the hood. They improve the engine's airflow and keep it cool.

The GT500 front air splitter works at high speeds to block airflow from lifting the car. The style hints at the 1968 Shelby GT500.

Shelby Cobra GT500 Then and Now

1967	**2007**
355 horsepower	450 horsepower
7-liter displacement	5.4-liter displacement
6 to 10 mpg	15 to 20 mpg

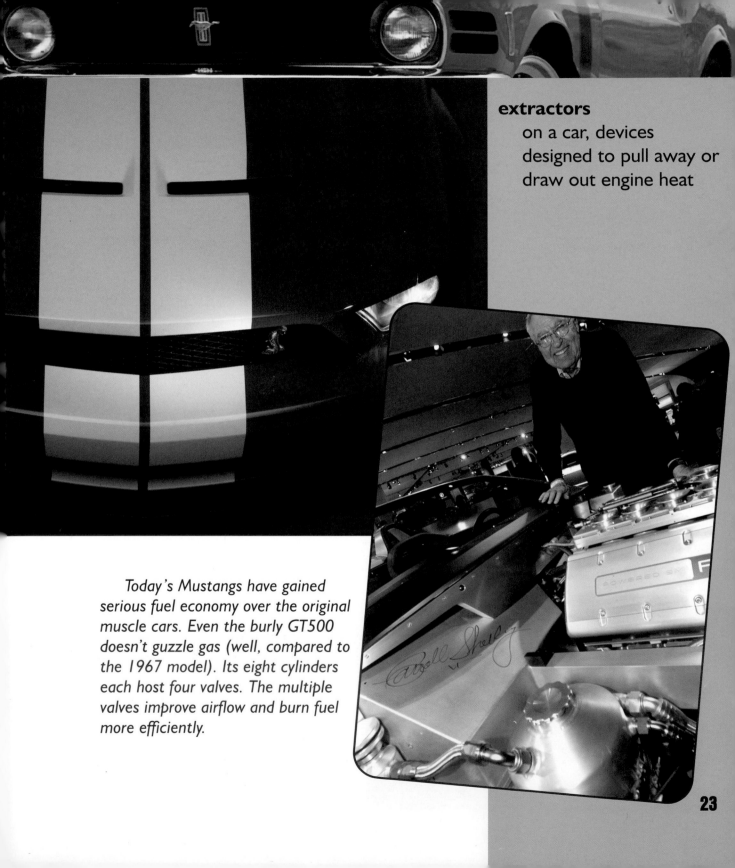

extractors
on a car, devices designed to pull away or draw out engine heat

Today's Mustangs have gained serious fuel economy over the original muscle cars. Even the burly GT500 doesn't guzzle gas (well, compared to the 1967 model). Its eight cylinders each host four valves. The multiple valves improve airflow and burn fuel more efficiently.

The Mustang GT and GT500 each have a dual exhaust system that gives the machines their throaty acceleration sound. Ford tunes the mufflers in a special laboratory.

Fast Fact

"FR" meant Ford Racing for the Mustang FR500C.

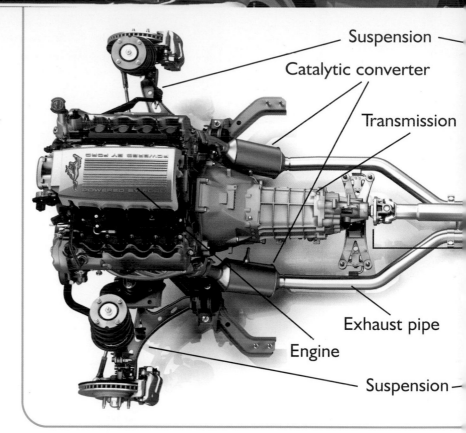

Suspension

Catalytic converter

Transmission

Exhaust pipe

Engine

Suspension

Not surprisingly, all the fifth-generation production Mustangs tapped ideas from the FR500C racer. The Shelby Cobra GT500 shares the same six-speed manual transmission and suspension as the winning FR500C car.

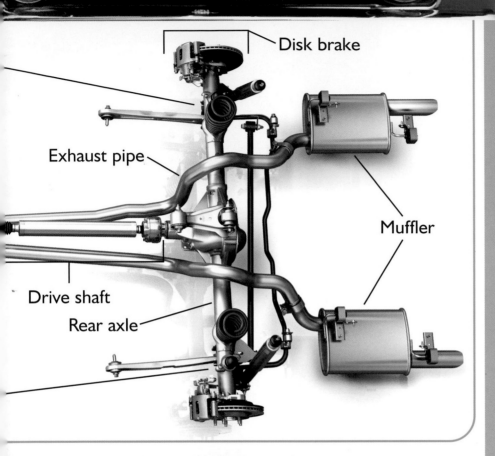

Disk brake

Exhaust pipe

Muffler

Drive shaft

Rear axle

rear-wheel drive
the engine drives the rear wheels, pushing the vehicle forward

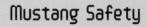

Mustang Safety

Modern Mustangs protect passengers like never before. Most muscle cars did not have seat belts. Now Mustangs can be fitted with driver and front-passenger side and front air bags.

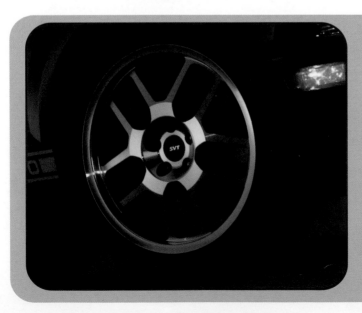

Today's Mustangs use **rear-wheel-drive** systems, just like the originals. The Shelby Cobra GT500 rides on mammoth 19-inch (48.25 cm) wheels and sports some of the biggest brakes on a factory-made street car.

Trophy Triumphs

In the 1960s, Fords collected trophies from road races, drag races, and just about any other race on four wheels. Carroll Shelby's name often had something to do with those trips down victory lane. With Shelby's nod, the Ford SVT engineers built the 1960-styled Mustang FR500C from the ground up to tackle Grand American Series "Gran Sport" class races. The new Mustang revved up the trophy trend again.

Skilled craftsmen build each race-ready Mustang FR500C by hand. They use the fifth-generation Mustang body style and a 5.0-liter "Cammer R50" engine that shares technology from the Mustang GT's 4.6-liter V-8.

The first Mustang FR500C arrived in its new garage just three days before winning its first-ever Grand Am race at the Daytona International Speedway 2005 season opener.

The Mustang FR500C is not a modified car pulled from the assembly line. So, it doesn't have a standard vehicle identification number (VIN). Instead, the Mustang FR500C has a catalog part number.

A customer can order the Mustang FR500C from the Ford Racing Performance Parts catalog. For about $125,000, the car comes with a race-ready roll cage, special brakes and suspension upgrades, and other safety equipment.

Fast Fact The FR500C is not **street legal.**

28

*Ford Racing Performance Parts sells **crate engines** and all the other parts needed to build a racecar from the ground up. Buyers can even order a fifth-generation Mustang "body-in-white" ready for the painter to spiff up in the team colors.*

Mustang "experts" are everywhere! According to Ford, Mustang fan clubs thrive on five continents. The car has appeared in more than 600 films and it's the focus of countless Web sites. As popular as ever, Mustang promises to deliver more driving fun down the road.

aftermarket
parts added to a vehicle after its sale to the owner

crate engines
new performance engines in shipping crates, ready for car owners to buy and install in their vehicles

street legal
a vehicle allowed to be driven on a city streets because it meets the standards set by law

Ford has built more than seven million Mustangs over the years.

Specialty 'Stangs

In 1984, specialty manufacturer Saleen built its first race-ready Mustan. It won eight GT manufacturer championships. Today, many companies like Saleen build or modify Mustangs. Roush Performance is one of the best-known manufacturers of high-performance **aftermarket** products for Mustangs.

Glossary

aftermarket (AFF tur MAR kit) – parts added to a vehicle after its sale to the owner

chassis (CHASS ee) – the frame that supports the body of a vehicle

coupe (KOOP) – a two-door car, usually with a solid roof

crate engines (KRAYT en JINZ) – new performance engines in shipping crates, ready for car owners to buy and install in their vehicles

extractors (ik STRAK tur) – on a car, devices designed to pull away or draw out engine heat

horsepower (HORS pow ur) – a measure of mechanical power; one horsepower equals 550 pounds (885 kg) lifted at one foot (30.5 cm) per second

muscle cars (MUSS ul KARZ) – generally, American cars built between 1964 and 1974 with big engines, two-doors, and back seats

mustang (MUSS tang) – a wild horse, especially in the American West

rear-wheel drive (REER WEEL drihv) – the engine drives the rear wheels, pushing the vehicle forward

street legal (STREET LEE gahl) – a vehicle allowed to be driven on a city streets because it meets the standards set by law

torque (TORK) – the force that causes an object to turn; usually measured in pound-ft (lb-ft)

V-8 (VEE ATE) – a motor with eight cylinders set in a V shape, each cylinder has a chamber that burns fuel

Further Reading

Henshaw, Peter. *Muscle Cars.* Thunder Bay Press,
San Diego, California. 2004.

Maurer, Tracy Nelson. *Roaring Rides: Muscle Cars*
Rourke Publishing, 2004.

Mezzanotte, Jim. *Story of the Ford Mustang*
Gareth Stevens Publishing, 2005.

Websites

www.fordvehicles.com/cars/mustang

www.fordracingparts.com/mustang/specifications.asp

www.muscularmustangs.com/index.php

www.mustangforums.com/ford/2007-gt500-mustang.asp

www.roushperf.com

Index

About the Author

Tracy Nelson Maurer writes nonfiction and fiction books for children, including more than 50 titles for Rourke Publishing LLC. Tracy lives with her husband Mike and two children near Minneapolis, Minnesota.